The FUNNY BEST MAN

Stewart Mair and Iain Mair

Copyright © 2013 by Stewart Mair and Iain Mair.

All rights reserved. No part of this book may be reproduced or transmitted in any form or by any means, electronic or mechanical, including photocopying, recording, or by any information storage and retrieval system, without permission in writing from the copyright owner.

This is a work of fiction. Names, characters, places and incidents either are the product of the author's imagination or are used fictitiously, and any resemblance to any actual persons, living or dead, events, or locales is entirely coincidental.

Contents

Why We Wrote this Book 5

Best Man Duties 7

Speech-Writing Tips 9

Speech Delivery 11

Order of Speeches 13

Best Man Speech Framework 15

    Introduction 15

    About the Groom 23

    Marriage Advice 37

    Apology Cards 41

    Toast 42

Example of Speeches 45

Why We Wrote This Book

Our purpose in writing this book was to help anyone faced with the prospect of being a best man succeed brilliantly. Most of the responsibilities that come with this special honor, which are listed below, are fairly straightforward. On the other hand, unless you're a professional public speaker or a natural extrovert, you're likely to find duty number 7—giving the best man speech at the reception—more than a little daunting (if not terrifying).

Unfortunately there's nothing we can do to help you with stage fright, except extend our condolences. However, what we can do is provide a framework to guide you in the creation of your speech and, most importantly, ensure that it contains some of the best jokes available. Based on our own experience as best men, and as guests at many weddings, we're convinced that humor is an essential part of the best man's speech. While we always encourage people to include as much original material as possible (poems, songs, etc.), this is not easy for everyone and it can be difficult to pull off successfully.

There is a mountain of information out there on being a best man. Our goal was to create a single, concise book that clearly summarizes the key responsibilities involved, and also contains a great selection of jokes that will guarantee a laugh from your audience. If you use the template below to structure your speech, add significant personal events or funny stories, and include the jokes that you feel will best appeal to the attendees, you'll succeed brilliantly.

Best Man Duties

1. Plan and organize the bachelor / stag party. This includes contacting friends, booking reservations, keeping everyone informed and generally dealing with the logistics.
2. If required, organize fittings for groomsmen and make sure everyone is properly attired.
3. Serve as a witness for the marriage license.
4. Help with transportation of guests to and from the wedding.
5. Assist with transportation of any needed items to the wedding and reception locations.
6. Hold the ring for the groom.
7. Give the best man speech at the reception (see below for typical order of speeches).
8. Dance with the maid of honor at the reception.
9. Return all formal wear after the wedding.

Speech-Writing Tips

1. Start working on your speech at least one month before the wedding (we would recommend even earlier). Begin by writing down all of the ideas that come into your head. Don't worry at this point if they seem silly or inappropriate—you can always decide not to use them later. In addition, ask family and friends for any relevant stories that can be included.
2. When you've collected all the information, choose the ideas and stories you like best and insert them in the appropriate sections of the framework we've provided below.
3. Be tactful and sensitive, and try not to lie.
4. Once everything is in place, review the speech in its totality and make any modifications that seem desirable.
5. Leave the speech for a couple of days, and then come back and make further modifications. Keep doing this until you are happy with it.

6. Once the speech is finalized, practice reading it out loud. Read it again and again until the words start becoming familiar.
7. We would also recommend reading it in front of one or more people, such as a friend or family member who is not attending the wedding.

Speech Delivery

1. If you are not accustomed to making speeches, bring a printed copy to the wedding so you can refer to it if needed. Alternatively, you can use cards that contain key components of the speech to help ensure that you don't lose your place.
2. Try not to be nervous. Everyone in the room will be supporting you. When it's your turn, be sure to stand up with a smile on your face.
3. Relax and take your time. A useful tip to help you relax is to begin the speech with one simple word before the opening sentence, such as "Hello", "Evening" or, as used in Example Best Man Speech 3, "Wow" to help ease you into the speech. This enables you to begin the speech and hear your own voice before you are tasked with the first full sentence.
4. Don't worry if you tell a funny story or joke and it doesn't get a laugh. In this case, just take a breath and carry on. One tip to deal with an awkward silence is to have a back up joke available, such as "I was testing

that gag for another best man. I'll just tell him to bin it."

5. If you start to feel that you're going on too long, don't be afraid to cut some things out.
6. Do not swear.
7. Be yourself.
8. Try not to drink too much before you speak (and try to make sure the groom is still sober as well).
9. Give it your best effort and try to enjoy the experience (it's a great honor to be asked).

Order of Speeches

Since guests are usually hungry after the wedding ceremony, the speeches normally come after the meal. The order is traditionally as follows:

1. If there is a Master of Ceremonies, he or she will speak first and introduce the speakers.
2. *Father of the Bride:* Welcomes guests and mentions those who could not make it and those who have travelled a long way. He will then talk fondly about his daughter and congratulate the groom on his choice of a wife. He will also talk about meeting the groom's family and might tell some stories about preparing for the wedding. The speech ends with a toast to the bride and groom.
3. *Groom:* The groom thanks his wife's father for welcoming him into the family and for the privilege of marrying his daughter. He will thank his parents for their support and guidance and thank the people who helped with the wedding preparations. He'll also thank the guests for attending and for their gifts, and

extend thanks to the best man and groomsmen for their support. He will then usually talk about his wife before proposing a toast to the bridesmaids.

4. *Best Man:* The best man thanks the bride and groom on behalf of the bridesmaids and himself for asking them to be part of their special day, and congratulates the bride and groom on their union. He then goes on to talk about the groom and his relationship with him. This is usually the high point in the speeches. As a general rule, it is recommended to keep in line with tradition of embarrassing the groom and praising the bride. Finally, he reads telegrams, cards, e-mails or other messages from friends and relatives who could not attend. It should be noted that the best man is not responsible for toasting the bride and groom.

Best Man Speech Framework

We have provided a broad selection of jokes and other speech components for you to choose from. Select the material that is most appropriate and will work best for the particular groom and wedding you are attending.

INTRODUCTION

At one wedding we attended, the best man pulled out a long piece of paper from his pocket, which took some time. Then he started reading: "Put cream on affected area." He looked up and said, "Oops, wrong piece of paper." This does need to be well acted.

In addition to selecting from the material here, include some information about how you know the groom.

Hello, ladies and gentlemen and distinguished guests. I use the words "distinguished guests" now as I probably won't be able to distinguish any of you later on tonight.

My name is [YOUR NAME] and for those of you who don't know me, I am the best man.

My name is [YOUR NAME] and, believe it or not, I am the best man.

I did try to memorize my speech, but I have a memory like a geriatric goldfish, so I'll be reading from my notes here. [THIS IS USEFUL IF ARE PLANNING ON READING YOUR NOTES DIRECTLY].

I'd like to thank [GROOM'S NAME] for his speech. I knew it would be hard to follow and I was right. I could hardly follow a word of it.

The Funny Best Man

I'd like to thank [GROOM'S NAME] for his compliments to the bridesmaids, all of which I heartily endorse.

On behalf of the bridesmaids, I would like to thank [GROOM'S NAME] for his kind words.

[IF YOU ARE SINGLE] Now I am sure the question on all the ladies' minds today is, "is that good-looking best man single?" Well, remarkably, the answer is yes. So, if you can send your applications up to the front, they'll be evaluated later tonight.

[IF YOU ARE SINGLE] Speaking as a single man myself—a very eligible single man, available for dates anytime, day or night . . . On this great day, I'm a little sad to see yet another woman taken off the market. Every single man will agree with this statement. Every single woman, on the other hand, will agree today is just another day.

[IF YOU ARE SINGLE] Good afternoon, ladies and gentlemen. It's wonderful to see two people so happy together with so much to look forward to. Me, I'm a bachelor by choice. Usually by the choice of the woman I have dated.

A wise man once said that a speech should last as long as the groom can make love—OK, goodnight, ladies and gentlemen.

[GROOM'S NAME] asked me if I would say a few words. He said not to say too much because he wants everyone to enjoy themselves.

Wedding protocol requires that the best man deliver a sober, clean and entertaining speech—and I sincerely hope that no one here is going to judge me against those unreasonable standards.

The Funny Best Man

⸻

I've really sweated and suffered over this speech and now it's your turn.

⸻

I just want to let you know that, to help my nervousness, I am picturing all of you in your underwear. Especially you, [NAME OF A GOOD-LOOKING <u>SINGLE</u> FEMALE].

⸻

I have to admit I'm very nervous about making this speech. To put my nervousness in perspective, this is the fifth time this afternoon that I've risen from a warm seat with a piece of paper in my hand.

⸻

I have to admit that I'm very nervous about making this speech. In fact, it reminds me of a story about the famous British admiral, Lord Nelson. He was asked why he always put on a red tunic before a battle. He said it was so the enemy wouldn't see the blood if he got injured. So, ladies and gentlemen, this explains why I am wearing brown underpants tonight.

I am a little nervous about making this speech. The last time I had to speak in public was at Alcoholics Anonymous. But I have to say, it's nice to see so many familiar faces here today.

When [GROOM'S NAME] asked me to be his best man, it was like being asked to sleep with the Queen of England. It's a great honor, but nobody really wants to do it.

[BROTHER] For those of you who don't know me, I'm [GROOM'S NAME]'s brother, [YOUR NAME]. It's great to be standing here today because, after all these years, [GROOM'S NAME] has finally admitted that I am the best man.

[BROTHER] In case you hadn't guessed, I'm [YOUR NAME], the groom's younger brother. Yes, it's true when artists say that they make a rough drawing before the final masterpiece.

I must admit I feel a little like I'm on trial here because [GROOM'S NAME] says if I do a good job, I can be the best man at his next wedding.

I'm actually quite excited about tonight as I've been told that, as part of my duties, I may need to do grace. So if anyone knows her whereabouts, can you let me know, because I haven't seen her all day.

While preparing for today, I decided to look online for some inspiration. It was a good idea. I spent two hours surfing the net and found lot of very good material—and I mean good material. It's just a shame I couldn't find anything on wedding speeches.

༺༻

They say the best man's speech is the groom's worst five minutes of the day. The bride's worst five minutes will come later tonight.

༺༻

I must say, [BRIDE'S NAME], that you just look stunning today. And [GROOM'S NAME], you just look a little stunned.

༺༻

I think you'll agree that [BRIDE'S NAME] looks stunning in that magnificent cream dress (ASSUMING THE BRIDE IS WEARING A CREAM DRESS). And of course [GROOM'S NAME]—you can at last say that your dish-washer now matches your fridge.

༺༻

ABOUT THE GROOM

In addition to selecting from the material here, include a few important events and/or funny stories about the groom.

Every now and again, we get the opportunity to talk about a man of the highest integrity and honor. A man of achievement and action, who is obviously destined for great things. Unfortunately, ladies and gentlemen, that is not going to happen today.

It's a wonderful honor to address a room full of people and speak in tribute to a man of high achievement, flawless integrity, piercing intellect and impeccable wit—and if I ever get that opportunity, I'll be sure to make the most of it.

As you know, the purpose of the best man's speech is to sing the groom's praises and point out all of his good qualities. Well, I don't sing and I won't lie.

It's customary to talk about all of the groom's past romantic conquests. [PAUSE] OK, that's done.

It's customary to talk about all of the groom's past girlfriends and romantic conquests. Since this would have added another two hours to the speech, I thought it best to just leave it out.

[GROOM'S NAME] has asked me to refrain from mentioning his past girlfriends. Sadly that's cut the speech short by a good three seconds.

[GROOM'S NAME] has asked me to refrain from mentioning his past girlfriends, which is fortunate since that's cut the speech by a good two hours.

The Funny Best Man

―⊙⋆⊙―

I'd like to take this time to talk about all of [GROOM'S NAME]'s accomplishments. I think we have time for both of them. First, he is a great speech writer, and second he is an amazing dancer. So play close attention to his dance moves later on, ladies and gentlemen.

―⊙⋆⊙―

Now, I'm not going to embarrass [GROOM'S NAME] too much. Because we all know he's quite capable of doing that himself.

―⊙⋆⊙―

[BRIDE'S NAME] contacted me before the wedding and asked me to help out on the wedding day to make sure it all goes smoothly. She mentioned three things that she wanted me to do:

- First, get him to the church on time. I think I achieved that.
- Second, make sure he's sober. I think I have done a reasonable job.

- Third, make sure he's looking good. Well, two out of three isn't too bad.

Anyone who knows [GROOM'S NAME] will know he is a skillful drinker. In fact, I can recall only one time that he spilled a drink. And that's also the only time I can remember seeing him cry.

People might ask if there is any difference in [GROOM'S NAME] since meeting [BRIDE'S NAME]. In fact, there is. Before, he was a big drinker. The difference now is that he has a beautiful woman sitting next to him.

[GROOM'S NAME] told [BRIDE'S NAME] that after the wedding he won't drink anymore. Mind you, he didn't say he would drink any less.

The Funny Best Man

❧

It's hard to believe, but [GROOM'S NAME] was a bit of a slow starter. But I'm glad to hear from [BRIDE'S NAME] that he's now a fast finisher.

❧

I have a lot of very good things to say about [GROOM'S NAME], as does everyone here today. He's generous, kind, industrious, charming, and the list goes on. However, I also heard one report that he's a bit lazy, stubborn, and can sometimes be a pain in the ass. Well, if [BRIDE'S NAME] doesn't know him, who does?

❧

I checked online to see if there were any major events going on the day [GROOM'S NAME] was born, but I couldn't find anything of significance. I did, however, find one small item reporting that the nurse at the local hospital called it "Ugly [DAY OF WEEK]."

They say marriage is made in heaven. Well, this one was made in McDonalds in [NAME OF LOCAL TOWN]. They do say it's quick and easy.

The other day, I was asking [GROOM'S NAME]'s father [FATHER'S NAME] about [GROOM'S NAME], and he was recalling him as a baby—hairy, plump and always wanting to be the center of attention. Come to think of it, he hasn't changed a bit.

Now some of you here may not know [GROOM'S NAME] very well. For example, you may not know about his nickname—"The Exorcist." That's because every time he comes around to visit, the spirits disappear.

Still, nobody has ever questioned [GROOM'S NAME]'s intelligence. In fact, I've never heard anyone mention it.

The Funny Best Man

⁘

Unfortunately, [GROOM'S NAME] and his mother-in-law [MOTHER-IN-LAW'S NAME] didn't get off to the best of starts. I remember, a while back, [GROOM'S NAME] and I went for a drink in [NAME OF LOCAL TOWN]. When we walked into the bar, there was [MOTHER-IN-LAW'S NAME] on the ground being beaten by six men. I asked [GROOM'S NAME], "Aren't you going to help?" He said, "No, six should be enough." But luckily they sorted it all out, and looking at them now, I think [GROOM'S NAME] has actually developed a soft spot for [MOTHER-IN-LAW'S NAME]. I believe it's a swamp just outside of [NAME OF LOCAL TOWN].

⁘

Now I am sure you will all agree that [BRIDE'S NAME] is looking stunning tonight. She is a lovely, caring person and deserves a special husband. [TO GROOM] Lucky for you, you married her before she found one.

⁘

I remember when [GROOM'S NAME] first saw [BRIDE'S NAME] and he wanted to go and ask her out. I was there at the time, and advised him to say to her that seeing her face made time stand still. He thought that was pretty good, so later that night, after, well, a few drinks, he went up to [BRIDE'S NAME] and said, "[BRIDE'S NAME], I have something to tell you." [BRIDE'S NAME] replied, "And what is that?" And he said, "Your face could stop a clock." So you can imagine how the romance blossomed from there.

As the wedding approached, [GROOM'S NAME] managed to stay pretty calm. The other night we had a few drinks with some friends and he stayed over at my house. And he slept like a baby. That's right, he wet the bed and woke up twice crying for his mommy.

[GROOM'S NAME] is a real charmer and in the early days he tried hard to impress [BRIDE'S NAME]. He took her out to a fancy restaurant, and the evening went very well. He made her laugh so hard, she dropped her fries.

I think the bride and groom complement each other very well. [BRIDE'S NAME] is ambitious, industrious, highly motivated and loves a challenge. And [GROOM'S NAME] is that challenge.

[SCOTTISH WEDDING] As you can see, [GROOM'S NAME] is wearing a kilt. Each tartan represents a different clan. I hear from [BRIDE'S NAME] that [GROOM'S NAME] is wearing a MacDonald tartan today. Apparently this is due to the chicken nugget underneath it.

The two of you are getting married for better or worse. Which is to say, [GROOM'S NAME] couldn't have done any better and [BRIDE'S NAME] couldn't have done any worse.

During my research, I looked into the three key elements of a wedding day: first, the aisle—the longest walk you'll ever take; second, the altar—the place where two become one; and third, the hymns, to celebrate the marriage. I hope for [GROOM'S NAME] sake that this explains why throughout the service [BRIDE'S NAME] was whispering "aisle, altar, hymn; I'll, alter, him".

There's no argument about who's going to be wearing the pants in [GROOM'S NAME] and [BRIDE'S NAME] house. [GROOM'S NAME] will be wearing them—right under his apron.

[SPORTS] [GROOM'S NAME] was telling me he plans to treat his marriage as seriously as he does his football. He says he's going in fully committed, plans to score every week, change ends at half time, and play half the season away from home. Although [BRIDE'S NAME] said if he does, he'll be in line for a serious groin injury.

[SPORTS] [GROOM'S NAME] is a big [NAME OF SPORT] fan, but his friends say as a player he was useless in every position. So let's hope the bride has a bit more luck.

∽⧫∾

I'd first like to say that [BRIDE'S NAME] looks absolutely fantastic today—one in a million. And [GROOM'S NAME], you look like you always do—won in a raffle.

∽⧫∾

Being the best man, it was my job to organize the stag party and take care of [GROOM'S NAME]. And he was a good sport. When we showed him his outfit, he put it on with no complaints—the mini-dress, earrings, make-up, high heels. Although, he refused to carry the handbag. He said it didn't go with his shoes.

∽⧫∾

We had a great time at the stag party. Although, there were a few things missing—there were no strippers, no lap dancing, no tying [GROOM'S NAME] naked to a lamp post. But as [GROOM'S NAME] said to me, "When you do that sort of thing every week, it's nice to take a break."

I really do believe that marriage will be a wonderful thing for [GROOM'S NAME]. It will teach him loyalty, self-restraint and control. And it will help him develop a sense of responsibility, fair play and so many other qualities he wouldn't need if he just stayed single.

I asked [GROOM'S NAME] what he was looking for in marriage. He said, "Love, happiness and eventually a family." When I asked [BRIDE'S NAME], she said "a toaster."

[GROOM'S NAME] and I attended school together and I remember he had a pretty rough time. He was constantly being picked on and getting beaten up. Although, I have to say, I didn't really blame the teachers at the time.

I was asking [BRIDE'S NAME] when she realized that it was time for her to get married, and she said it was one night in [MONTH, YEAR], when she finally met the man of her dreams—he was handsome, well-educated and just a great guy. Well, it was a couple of weeks after that she met [GROOM'S NAME].

Today is all about the happy couple, and don't they look great. [BRIDE'S NAME] looks wonderful and [GROOM'S NAME], well, they sure knew how to make a suit in the 1990s.

[BRIDE'S NAME] is just wonderful—beautiful, intelligent, caring. And I think, in [GROOM'S NAME], she's made a wonderful choice of a first husband.

In the old days, [GROOM'S NAME] and I couldn't walk into a bar without gorgeous women annoying us all night. That is, none of them would talk to us.

What I like best about [GROOM'S NAME] is that you can talk to him about any subject. He doesn't understand, but you can talk to him.

Since getting engaged, [BRIDE'S NAME] maintained that she wanted a quiet, simple wedding. And that's what she got, starting with the groom.

The first time [GROOM'S NAME] set eyes on [BRIDE'S NAME] he was knocked out by her looks. She was drop-dead gorgeous. "You're gorgeous," he said. "Drop dead," she told him.

Being a staunch traditionalist, [GROOM'S NAME] did the time-honored, decent thing when it came to proposing to [BRIDE'S NAME]. He went down on one knee—and then he went down on the other. And then he begged [NAME OF BRIDE'S FATHER] to pay for the wedding.

I've known [GROOM'S NAME] for many years and in some ways you could say I've been like a father to him. I saw him drink from a bottle, I watched him try to walk, I dressed and undressed him and cleaned up after him . . . and that was just last night.

MARRIAGE ADVICE

May you live each day like your last and each night like your first.

I asked a friend of mine what the secret is to a good marriage. He said that it's important to go out twice a week to a nice restaurant, have a good bottle of wine, maybe do some dancing and end the night with some wild romance. He said he goes on Thursdays and his wife goes on Saturdays.

[TO BRIDE] All you have to remember is that a husband is like a tiled floor. Lay it right the first time and you can spend years walking all over it.

I have some marital advice for the young couple, and that is to remember the five rings: the engagement ring, the wedding ring, the suffering, the enduring and the torturing.

You need to set the ground rules and establish who is boss. Then, [GROOM'S NAME], do everything [BRIDE'S NAME] says.

Never forget to tell your wife those three important little words: "I was wrong."

Now that you're married, I'd like to remind you that there are three types of sex in a marriage—all-over-the-house sex, bedroom sex and hallway sex. All-over-the-house sex occurs in the first year or so of marriage. It's when you'll do it anytime, anywhere, in any position for any reason. Bedroom sex follows this wild period, which is when you'll have sex on a Saturday night (if you're lucky) in the bedroom. Hallway sex comes later in the marriage. This is when you pass each other in the hallway and scream, "Screw you!"

They say in the first year of marriage, the man speaks and the woman listens. In the second year, the woman speaks and the man listens. In the third year, they both speak and the neighbors listen.

[TO BRIDE] Remember that men are like fine wine. Like grapes, you need to stomp on them until they mature into something special. [TO GROOM] And women are also like fine wine. They start off fresh, fruity and intoxicating. Then they turn full-bodied, and then a little sour and vinegary. And in the end, they just give you a headache.

[BRIDE'S NAME]—I have four pieces of advice for you:

1. Make sure you've got a man who doesn't mind helping at home.
2. Make sure you've got a man with a good sense of humor.
3. Make sure you've got a man that is dependable and has no secrets.
4. But, most importantly of all, make sure [GROOM'S NAME] doesn't find out about any of these men.

For inspiration, I decided to look to the Big Man himself. And as Homer Simpson would say, marriage is like being married to your best friend, only she lets you touch her boobs.

[TO GROOM] I have to say how lucky you are, [GROOM'S NAME]. You will leave here today having gained a wife who is warm, loving and caring. Someone who is funny and brightens up the place wherever she goes.

[TO BRIDE] And, [BRIDE'S NAME], how lucky you are as well. [PAUSE] You leave today having gained a [PAUSE] gorgeous dress and a lovely bouquet of flowers.

APOLOGY CARDS

I am almost at the end of my speech and I have one more duty to perform, which is to read letters and cards from people who are unable to be with us today.

In addition to reading the real cards, you may want to include one or both of the following:

To [GROOM'S NAME],

Have a great day, and thanks for your generosity over the years.

All the dancers at [NAME OF LOCAL STRIP CLUB].

To [BRIDE'S NAME],

I am so sorry . . . Oh, that seems to be all it says.

TOAST

Well, I'm almost done, ladies and gentlemen. I won't keep you much longer as I know [GROOM'S NAME] is dying to buy you all a drink at the bar.

It's been an honor today being the best man and this is my favorite duty—to propose a toast to the newlyweds. Can you please raise your glasses—to love, life, laughter and a happy ever after.

Anyway I have kept you all long enough, so would you please raise your glasses and toast. To the bar staff.

The Funny Best Man

So please would you join with me in wishing [GROOM'S NAME] and [BRIDE'S NAME] the very best in the future. I am sure they will be very happy together.

And now, ladies and gentlemen, the time has come for me to ask you all to fill your glasses and join me in a toast to the future welfare and happiness of the bride and groom.

And finally, in closing, to [BRIDE'S NAME] and [GROOM'S NAME]: May all your ins and outs, and ups and downs, be in the bedroom.

Example of Speeches

EXAMPLE 1 BEST MAN SPEECH

Hello, ladies and gentlemen.

As you know, the purpose of the best man's speech is to sing the groom's praises and point out all of his good qualities. Well, I don't sing and I won't lie.

It's customary to talk about all of the groom's past romantic conquests. [PAUSE] OK, that's done.

I have to admit that I'm very nervous about making this speech. To put my nervousness in perspective, this is the fifth time this afternoon that I've risen from a warm seat with a piece of paper in my hand.

Margo contacted me before the wedding and asked me to help out on the wedding day to make sure it all goes smoothly. She mentioned three things that she wanted me to do:

- First, get him to the church on time. I think I achieved that.
- Second, make sure he's sober. I think I have done a reasonable job.
- Third, make sure he's looking good. Well, two out of three isn't bad.

But you know, the other day, I was asking John's father about John, and he said he remembers him as a baby—hairy, plump and always wanting to be the center of attention. Come to think of it, he hasn't changed much in 34 years.

Speaking as a single man myself—a very eligible single man, available for dates anytime, day or night . . . On this great day, I'm a little sad to see yet another woman taken off the market. Every single man will agree with this statement. Every single woman, on the other hand, will agree today is just another day.

I've been good friends with John over the years. We met in the Kilmaurs Young Farmers Club, where we developed a taste for women and beer. We were much more successful with the beer than the women. In the early days, we used to go drinking quite a lot at the Fenwick Hotel, usually after the Young Farmer concert practices. John became quite

The Funny Best Man

famous locally and many people would turn up to watch his party trick—the star jump. If you're lucky, we'll maybe get to see it later on tonight.

In our Young Farmer days, our drinking crowd consisted of Alastair and Iain Mair, Jason McBurnie, Billy Smith, John Cameron and Paul Littlejohn, all of whom are here today. We were known to the ladies as the good-looking group. And those of you who don't know Paul Littlejohn, you may have heard of his nickname—"The Exorcist." Because every time he comes to visit, the spirits disappear.

I have a lot of very good things to say about John, as does everyone here today. He's generous, kind, industrious, charming, and the list goes on. However, I also heard one report that he's a bit lazy and stubborn, and can sometimes be a real pain in the ass. Well, if Margo doesn't know him, who does?

Still, nobody has ever questioned John's intelligence . . . . In fact I've never heard anyone mention it.

I'm sure you'll agree John and Margo make a lovely couple and are well suited. John and Margo have been living together for some time and John was telling me he remembers when Margo got insured for his beloved Zetor tractor. Within one month, he needed to get the clutch replaced. He came home and mentioned this to Margo, who said, "Don't look at me, I never use it."

Ladies and gentlemen, they say love is made in heaven. In this case it was the Spar Car Park in Stewarton. They do say it's quick and easy.

Unfortunately, John didn't get off to the best of starts with his mother-in-law, Ann. I remember a while back John and I went for a drink in Kilmarnock. When we walked into the bar, there was Ann on the ground being beaten by six men. I asked John, "Aren't you going to help?" He said, "No, six should be enough."

But luckily they sorted it all out, and looking at them now I think John has actually developed a soft spot for Ann. I think it's a swamp outside Stewarton.

Well, I'm almost done, ladies and gentlemen. I won't keep you much longer as I know John is dying to buy you all a drink at the bar.

I do have to say how lucky you are, John. You will leave here today having gained a wife who is warm, loving and

The Funny Best Man

caring. Someone who is funny, and brightens up the place wherever she goes.

And Margo, how lucky you are as well. [PAUSE] You leave today having gained a [PAUSE] gorgeous dress and a lovely bouquet of flowers.

It's been an honor today being the best man and, John, I know I made a lot of jokes, but to be serious for a moment—I do think you are a very lucky man and you both make a lovely couple.

Now for my favorite duty today—I'd like to propose a toast to the newlyweds. Can you please raise your glasses—to love, laughter, Zetors and a happy ever after. To John and Margo.

EXAMPLE 2 BEST MAN SPEECH

Colin has asked me if I would say a few words. He said not to say too much because he wants people to enjoy themselves. So I will keep it short.

I haven't known Colin all my life, but the other day I was talking to his mum about him, and she was saying she remembers how, as a baby, he was hairy, plump and always wanting to be the center of attention. Come to think of it, 27 years later he hasn't changed a bit.

As I lived with Colin for a while and know him pretty well, Michelle asked me to help out on the wedding day and make sure everything goes smoothly. She mentioned three things that she wanted me to do:

- First, get him to the registry office on time. I think I achieved that.
- Second, make sure he's sober. I think I have done a reasonable job.
- Third, make sure he's looking good. Well, two out of three isn't bad.

I have to admit that I'm very nervous about making this speech. It reminds me of a story about the famous British admiral, Lord Nelson. He was asked why he always put on a red tunic before a battle. He said it was so the enemy wouldn't see the blood if he got injured.

This explains why I'm wearing brown underpants tonight.

Anyway, I'm sure you'll all agree that Michelle is looking stunning tonight. She is a lovely, caring person and deserves a special husband. Lucky for you, Colin, you married her before she found one.

Now Michelle, all you have to remember is that a husband is like a tiled floor. [PAUSE] Lay it right the first time and you can spend years walking all over it.

Back when I lived with Colin, he was a big football fan and he used to play every Monday night—but his teammates said he was useless in every position . . . so let's just hope the bride has better luck.

Anyway, I was trying to remember the day Colin and Michelle met. And it was actually at the Highland show. But Michelle was a bit nervous about speaking to him, so she asked my advice. I suggested she just go straight up to Colin and say, "Colin, seeing your face makes time stand still." She thought that was pretty good, and so later that night—she'd had a few and was a little confused—she went up to Colin and said, "Colin, I have something to tell you." And Colin replied, "What's that?" And she said, "Your face could stop a clock." So you can imagine how the romance blossomed.

The other hurdle to get over was for Colin to meet Michelle's mother. Unfortunately Colin and Patricia didn't get off to the best of starts. For example, I remember one time Colin and I went for a drink at this kind of rough bar, and when we walked in, there was his mother-in-law being beaten by six men.

I asked him, "Aren't you going to help?"

To which Colin replied, "No, six should be enough."

But luckily they sorted it all out, and actually looking at them now, I think Colin has developed quite a soft spot for Tricia . . . I think it's a swamp outside Dundonald, right?

In the buildup to the wedding, Colin has been amazingly calm. In fact, the other night we had a few too many drinks and so he stayed over at my place. And he slept like a little baby. That's right, he wet the bed and woke up crying for his mommy!

Still, nobody has ever questioned Colin's intelligence . . . . In fact I have never heard anyone mention it.

Almost done, ladies and gentlemen. I wont keep you much longer as I know Colin is dying to buy you all a drink at the bar.

Before I carry on, Michelle, would you place your right hand on the table. And, Colin, would you place your left hand on top of hers.

Now, I have some marital advice for the young couple. First of all, remember the five rings:

The engagement ring, the wedding ring, the suffering, the enduring and the torturing.

Next, be sure to set the ground rules to establish who's the boss. Then, Colin, do everything Michelle says.

And always remember to tell your wife those three important little words: [PAUSE] "I was wrong."

Anyway, I have kept you all long enough, so would you please raise your glasses and toast . . . . To the bar staff. [START TO SIT DOWN]

Wait a minute, sorry, there's a bit more.

I do have to say how lucky you are, Colin. You will leave here having gained a wife who is warm, loving and caring. A wife who is funny, and who brightens up every place she goes.

And Michelle, how lucky you are as well. [PAUSE] You leave today having gained a [PAUSE] gorgeous dress and a lovely bouquet of flowers.

Now, in case any of you are wondering why I asked Colin to place his hand on Michelle's, I'll tell you now. Colin, it has been my pleasure to give you these five minutes during which you have had the upper hand with Michelle. It will almost certainly be the last time.

So please would you join me in wishing Colin and Michelle the very best in the future. I am sure they will be very happy together.

To Colin and Michelle.

FAKE APOLOGY CARDS:

To Colin,

Have a great day, and thanks for your kind generosity over the years.

All the dancers at Legs and Co.

To Michelle,

I am so sorry . . . Oh, that seems to be all it says!

EXAMPLE 3 BEST MAN SPEECH

Wow! It's finally happened! It only took Stewart 35 years, but he has finally admitted that, yes, I am the best man!

Good afternoon, ladies and gentlemen. In case you hadn't guessed, I'm Iain, the groom's younger brother. Yes, it's true when artists say that they make a rough drawing before the final masterpiece.

I originally had quite a long speech, but then Stewart asked me to refrain from mentioning any of his past girlfriends, so the speech now . . . well, to be honest, it's pretty much the same length.

During my research, I looked into the three key elements of a wedding day: first, the aisle—the longest walk you'll ever take; second, the altar—the place where two become one; and third, the hymns—to celebrate the marriage. I hope for Stewart's sake that this explains why throughout the service Elizabeth was whispering, "Aisle, altar, hymn; I'll, alter, him"!

Nice to see so many friends from across the pond. I hope you are all enjoying a traditional Scottish wedding, with the beautiful bride Elizabeth in white and of course Stewart in the traditional kilt.

For those of you that are not familiar with the kilt, each tartan, or plaid pattern, represents a different clan. Just to clear up any confusion, I would like to confirm that Stewart is wearing the Smith tartan. I believe Elizabeth may have been informing people that it was the MacDonald. This was apparently due to the chicken nugget underneath it.

It's actually quite fitting that Stewart is wearing a dress today, since pretty much from tomorrow onwards, it will be Elizabeth who's wearing the pants.

With regard to the stag party, I'm afraid I have to stick to the rule about "what happens in Vegas stays in Vegas." But just to give you an idea, it involved tequila shots, dancing on tables with scantily dressed women and, of course, strippers. Unfortunately Stewart never got to see any of this, as he was passed out in bed by 6:00 pm.

I would just like to mention the bridesmaids, who I am sure you will agree look wonderful and performed their role fantastically, despite the inevitable rivalry that tends to come up. In fact, just before the service, I overheard a heated argument about who was going to be first to dance with the best man. Of course I was flattered—until I got closer and heard them saying, "You!" "No, you!"

Another traditional duty for the best man is to give advice to the happy couple. So, Elizabeth, I have four pieces of advice for you:

1. Make sure you've got a man who doesn't mind helping at home.
2. Make sure you've got a man with a good sense of humor.
3. Make sure you've got a man that is dependable and has no secrets.
4. But, most importantly of all, make sure Stewart doesn't find out about any of these men.

So please would you join with me in wishing Stewart and Elizabeth the very best in the future. I am sure they will be very happy together.

Printed in Great Britain
by Amazon